WHO WAS NICOLAUS COPERNICUS?

****

A VERY SHORT INTRODUCTION ON SPACE GRADE 3 | CHILDREN'S BIOGRAPHIES

DISSECTED LIVES
auto biographies

DISSECTED LIVES

First Edition, 2019

Published in the United States by Speedy Publishing LLC, 40 E Main Street, Newark, Delaware 19711 USA.

© 2019 Dissected Lives Books, an imprint of Speedy Publishing LLC

Dissected Lives Books are available at special discounts when purchased in bulk for industrial and sales-promotional use. For details contact our Special Sales Team at Speedy Publishing LLC, 40 E Main Street, Newark, Delaware 19711 USA. Telephone (888) 248-4521 Fax: (210) 519-4043. www.speedybookstore.com

10 9 8 7 6 * 5 4 3 2 1

Print Edition: 9781541952881
Digital Edition: 9781541955882

See the world in pictures. Build your knowledge in style.
https://www.speedypublishing.com/

CONTENTS

★★

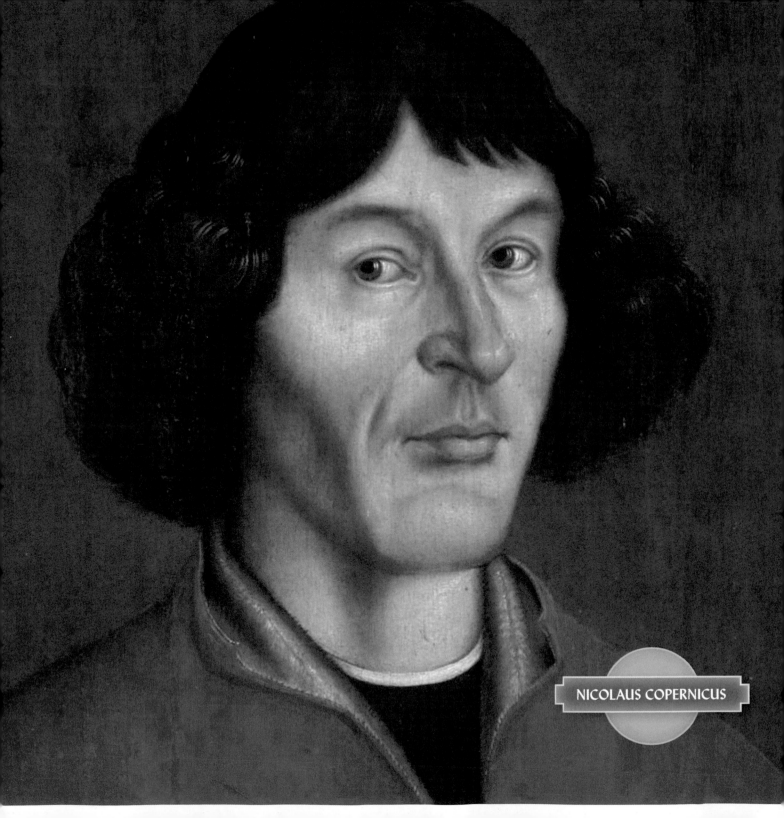

NICOLAUS COPERNICUS

In this book, we're going to talk about the life and theories of astronomer Nicolaus Copernicus, so let's get right to it!

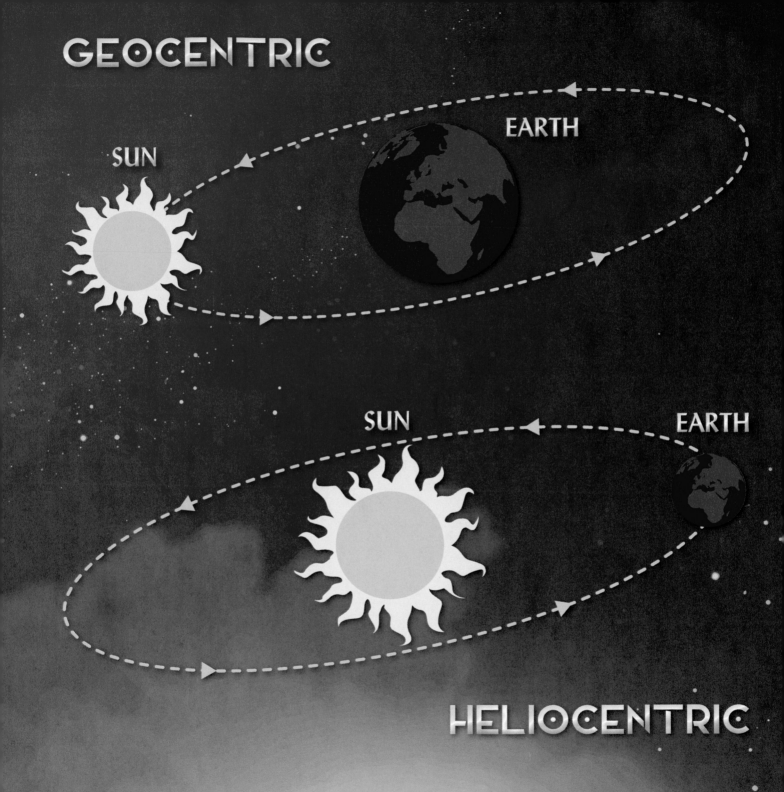

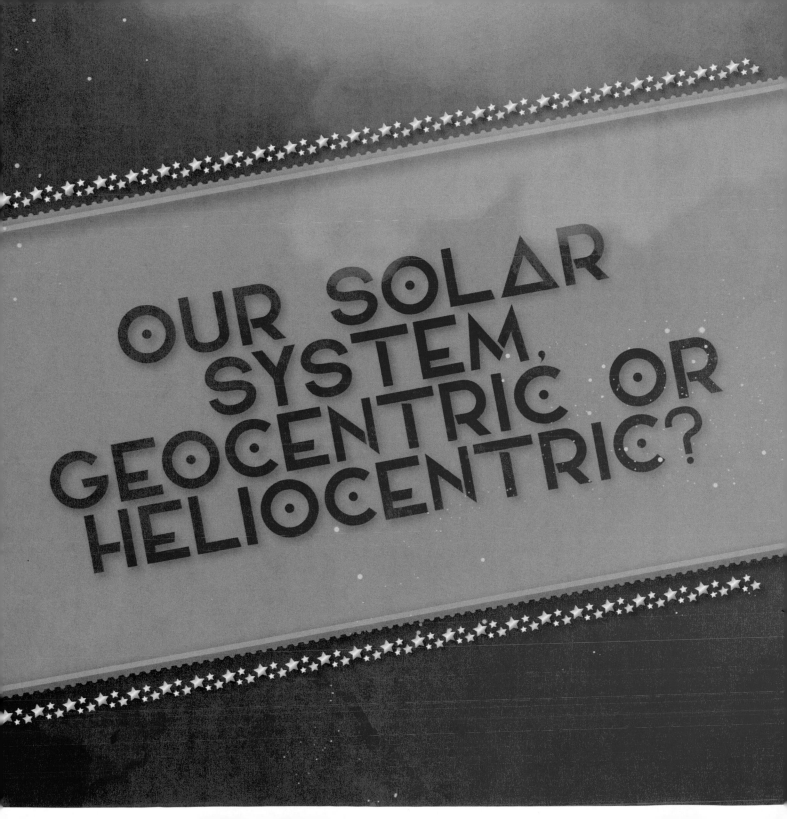

As human beings looked up at the sky for thousands of years, they felt that the Earth was the center of the solar system, perhaps even of the entire universe. Today, we call this theory the geocentric theory of the solar system, which simply means the Earth-centered model.

GEOCENTRIC MODEL OF THE UNIVERSE

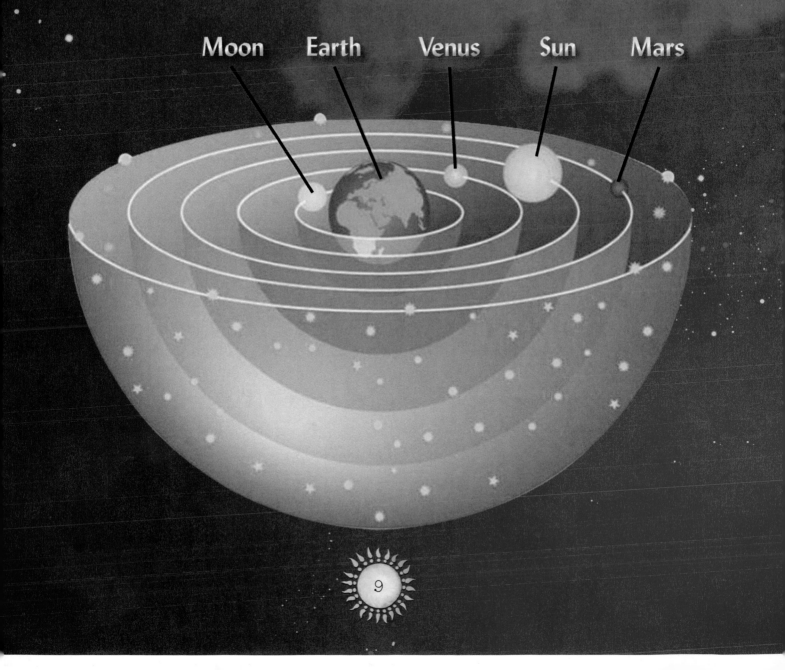

Moon Earth Venus Sun Mars

Ancient
peoples began
to notice that
there were certain
celestial bodies
that were bright and
seemed to move against the
background of the stars.

No one knows exactly
who discovered that
these celestial bodies were
planets. They could be viewed
without the aid of a telescope.
Cultures worldwide eventually began
to notice and record them.

Jupiter

Mars

During the time of ancient Greek civilization, the
"naked-eye" planets in order from Mercury to Saturn
had been named. Planet Earth was thought
to be in the center of it all with the
others revolving around it.

Saturn

Venus

Mercury

However, not everyone in Greece believed this. An astronomer called Aristarchus of Samos was one of the first to theorize that the Sun might be at the core of the known universe. But, the idea that the Earth was at the universe's center was so fundamentally believed that no one took the idea of the Sun at the center seriously. It wasn't brought up again until centuries later.

ARISTARCHUS
OF SAMOS

ANTICOENHC

ARISTOTLE

Much of Europe used Greek research for their knowledge and the teachings of famous Greek scholars such as philosopher and scientist Aristotle (367 BCE to 347 BCE) and the Greco-Roman astronomer Ptolemy (100 CE to 170 CE) aligned with the view that the Earth was the center of what we now call the solar system.

However, by the sixteenth century, there were challenges with astronomy that prompted some changes in thinking. Tables and charts based on astronomical measurements were becoming inaccurate. These were used for navigation and also for the yearly calendar. Several astronomers began to dig through the ancient Greek texts to discover errors.

This knowledge was used by Nicolaus Copernicus to explain a different, and accurate, model of the solar system. This model was called the heliocentric model because the Sun was at its center. Because of his important contributions, Copernicus is thought of as the father of modern astronomy.

HELIOCENTRIC MODEL OF THE UNIVERSE

TORUN, THE BIRTHPLACE OF
NICOLAUS COPERNICUS

The youngest of four children, Nicolaus Copernicus was born in February of 1473 in Poland. His father was a wealthy merchant and his mother also came from a family of merchants who were also quite wealthy. His father passed away when he was young and his mother's brother, his uncle, raised him.

JAGIELLONIAN UNIVERSITY
IN KRAKÓW, POLAND

His uncle was a Roman Catholic bishop and he sent Nicolaus to the university in Kraków, Poland for his studies. Copernicus was a polymath. That simply means that he excelled in many different types of fields. He studied astronomy as well as astrology, which at that time were connected to each other.

He also traveled to Italy to study law and medicine. After his years in the university, he became an administrative official in the Catholic Church. By the time he was twenty-seven he was teaching mathematics in Rome, but he came back to the family's castle in Frombork, Poland around 1507 to take care of his elderly uncle.

He spent every spare evening and night researching the night sky. He began to compile his research so that he could publish his findings in a book.

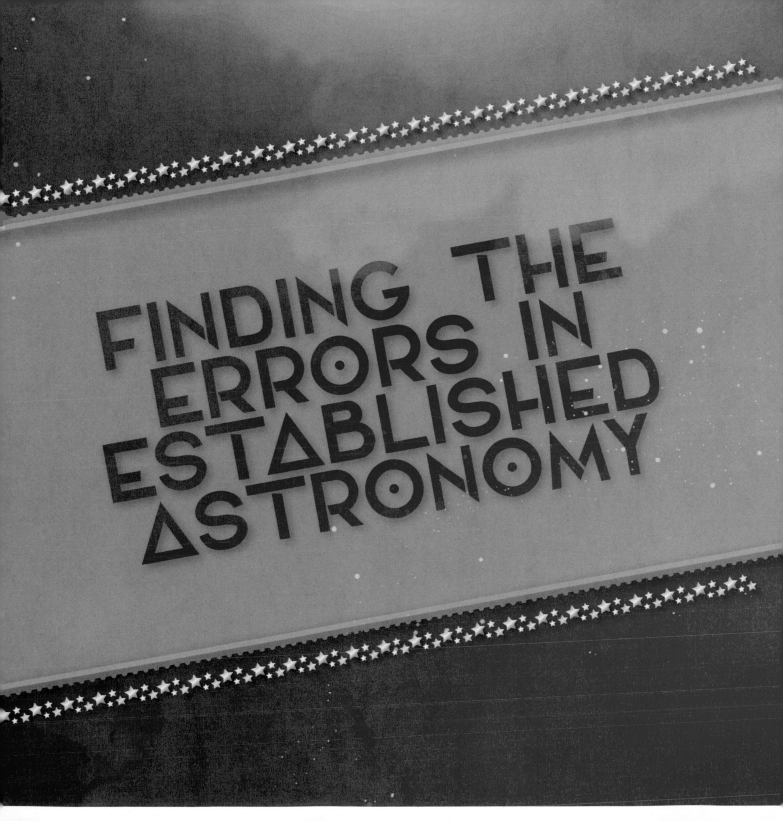

FINDING THE ERRORS IN ESTABLISHED ASTRONOMY

While Copernicus had been in Italy, he had worked with Domenico Maria Novara, who was a master astronomer. They had watched the sky together on countless nights. In a sense, Copernicus was acting as an apprentice to the more experienced astronomer.

COPERNICUS WAS ACTING AS AN APPRENTICE TO DOMENICO MARIA NOVARA

In those days, there were no telescopes. The first man to look at the night sky with a telescope was Galileo Galilei and by the time he did this, it was twenty years after Copernicus had died.

GALILEO GALILEI

JOHANNES REGIOMONTANUS

Copernicus was using a book written by an astronomer called Johannes Regiomontanus. The book was a summary of Ptolemy's masterwork called *Almagest*, which had been considered the top reference in astronomy for many centuries. The book had been brought to Europe from the Arab countries and it had been translated from the Greek language to Arabic and then to Latin.

Regiomontanus thought that these translations had introduced errors into Ptolemy's work. So, to solve this problem, he found *Almagest* in the original Greek and had it translated directly to Latin. He was shocked to find out that the mistakes weren't errors in translation. They were mistakes in the original book!

Laus Deo optimo marimoqz

Petrus   Liechtenstein

Contigimus portum: quo modo cursus erat.
Hic teneat nostras : ancora iacta rates.
1 5 1 5

In Ptolemy's original calculations, the moon's distance to the Earth would change by a factor of two. That would mean that the size of the moon would sometimes be half of its size in the sky compared to its full size at other times. But, this didn't make sense with what was actually observed in the sky.

So, as Copernicus worked with Novara, he began to collect some ideas:

⭐ The work of Regiomontanus had made it clear that Ptolemy had made calculation errors in his original work.

⭐ Novara, his mentor, had agreed that Ptolemy's work had errors.

⭐ He had read the work of other Italian scholars, such as Alessandro Achillini, who had stated that Ptolemy's work had significant mistakes.

ALESSANDRO ACHILLINI

As Copernicus thought about Ptolemy's theories he realized that they could be completely wrong and that the Earth might not be at the center of the heavens at all. It was shocking to think about.

EARTH MIGHT NOT BE AT THE
CENTER OF THE HEAVENS AT ALL

COPERNICUS IS SHOWN AT WORK IN A 20TH-CENTURY PAINTING

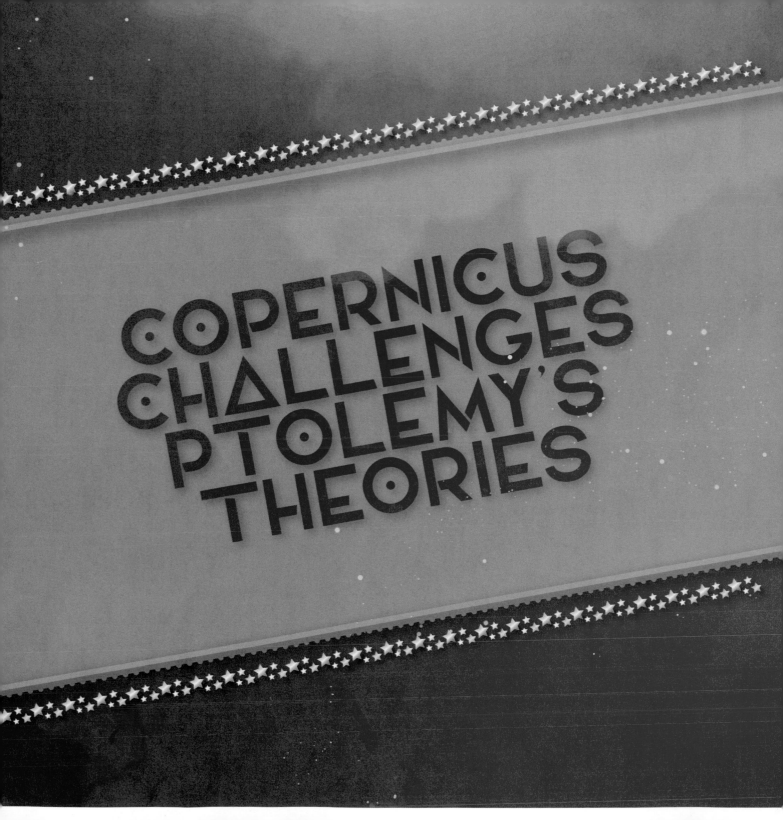
COPERNICUS CHALLENGES PTOLEMY'S THEORIES

For more than 1400 years, Ptolemy's Theory that the Earth didn't move and that it was at the center as the planets and the Sun revolved around it was the accepted theory. At first, the common thinking was that the other planets went around the Earth in circular paths called orbits. But, the calculations from viewing the skies didn't match up with this model. Then, it was thought that each planet traveled in smaller circular paths within those larger circular orbits. Even though this idea matched better with actual observations, it still wasn't proof that the Earth was at the center.

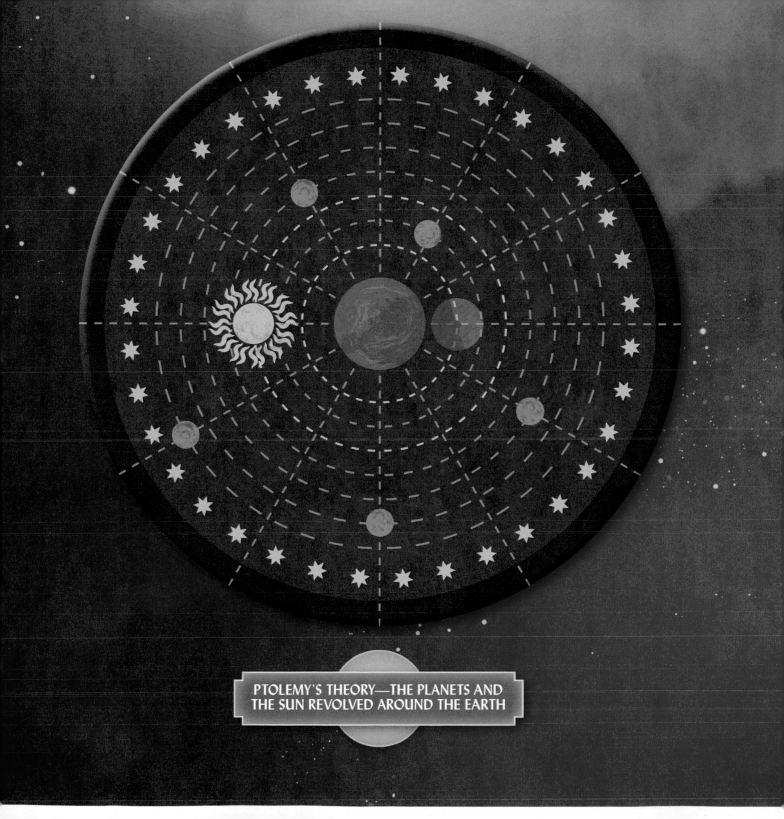

PTOLEMY'S THEORY—THE PLANETS AND
THE SUN REVOLVED AROUND THE EARTH

ILLUSTRATION OF THE COPERNICAN SYSTEM

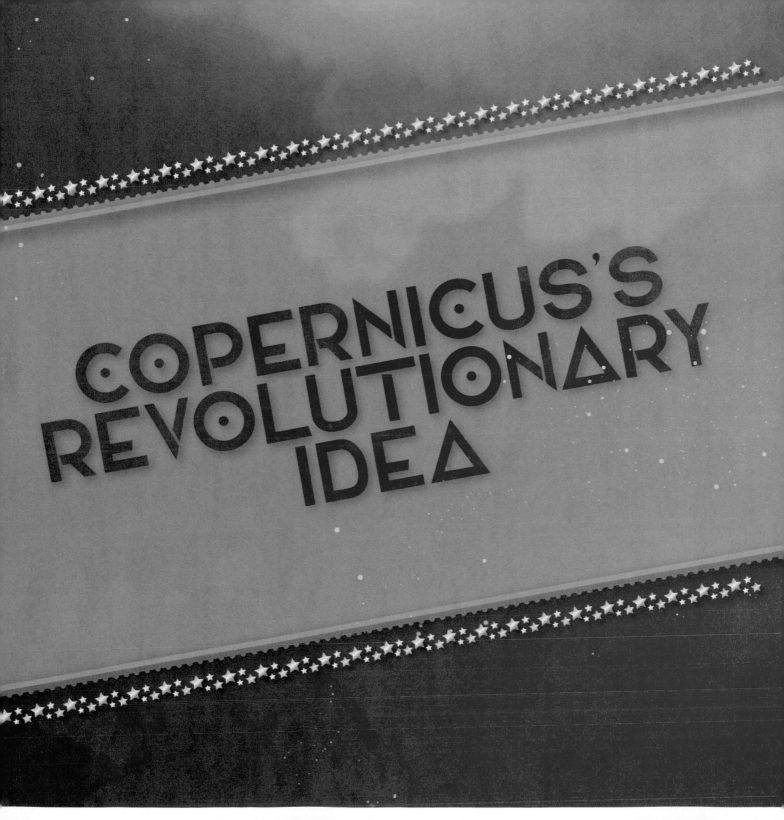

COPERNICUS'S REVOLUTIONARY IDEA

No one knows exactly when Copernicus realized that the 1400 years of ingrained thinking was absolutely incorrect. Sometime between the years 1508 and 1514 he realized where his observations were leading. He felt certain that the Sun, a star, was at the center and that the Earth was a planet like the others. The planets revolved around the Sun.

THE PLANETS REVOLVED
AROUND THE SUN

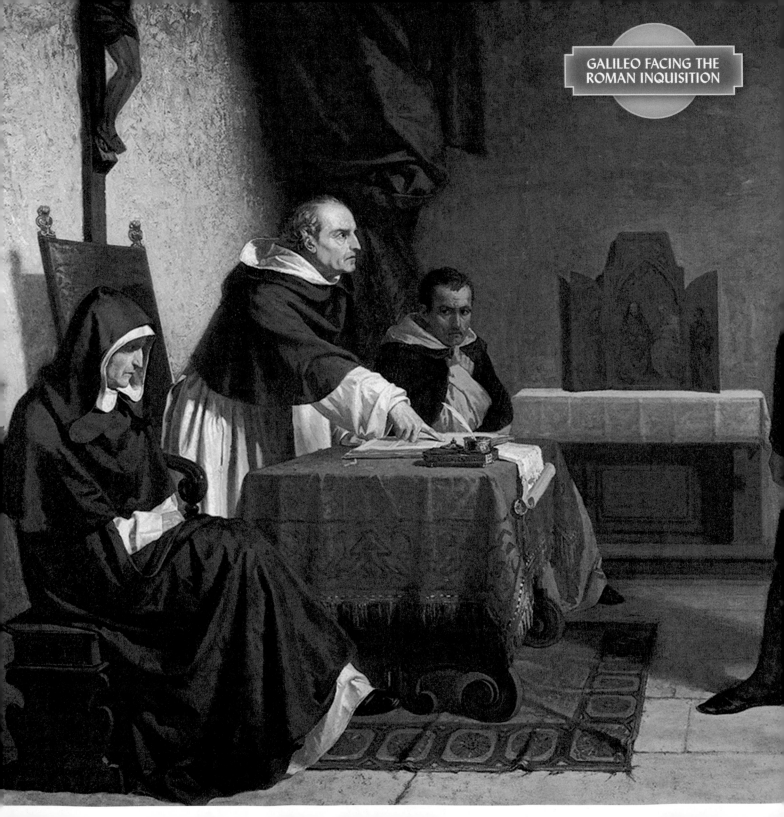

He also theorized that the Earth spun on its axis. However, he still held to the idea that the planets had smaller circular orbits along the larger orbit paths, which was incorrect. He knew that his theories would be difficult for people to accept. He was aware that the Roman Catholic Church would be against his scientific views. So, he delayed getting his findings published. Later on, after Copernicus's death, the astronomer Galileo Galilei agreed with Copernicus's findings and the Catholic Church persecuted him as a result.

BRONZE MONUMENT OF NICOLAUS COPERNICUS AT ENTRANCE TO THE CASTLE IN OLSZTYN

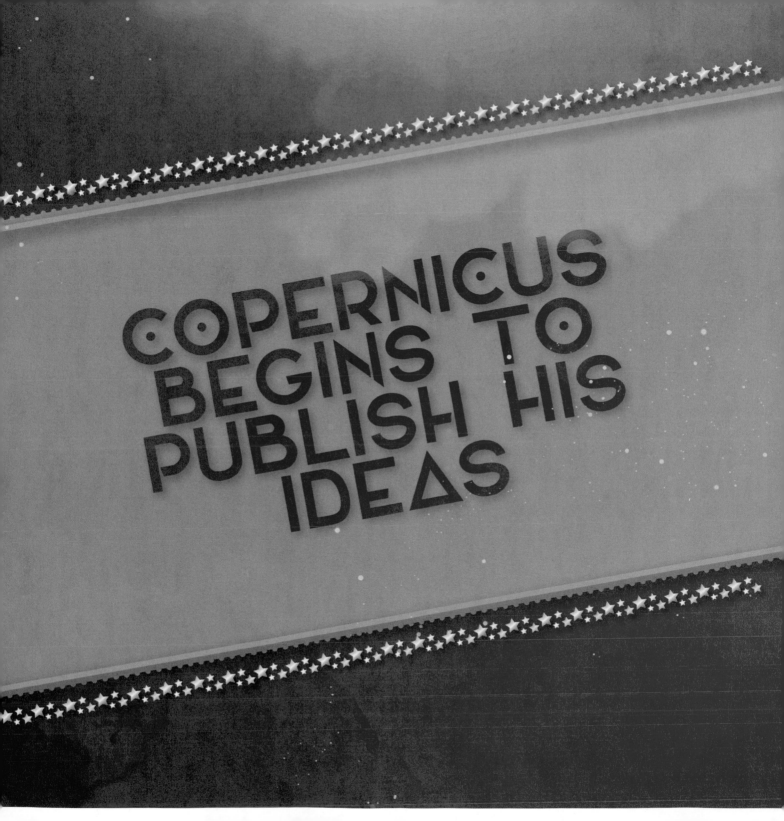

COPERNICUS BEGINS TO PUBLISH HIS IDEAS

Nicolai Copernici

de Hypothesibus motuum coelestium
à se ceris titulis
commentariolus.

COMMENTARIOLUS

By the time Copernicus was in his early forties, he started to publish his ideas. At first, he was careful about it. He put a small, handwritten document together, which he called the *w*. This little commentary put forth his major theory that people should think of the planets traveling around the Sun not the Earth.

He stated that:

★ The Earth wasn't the center of what we now consider the solar system.

★ The distance between the Earth and the Sun was insignificant compared to their distance from the stars.

★ The stars look like they are rotating daily because the Earth is spinning on its own axis.

★ The Sun isn't moving, but it seems like it is because the Earth is traveling around it.

He realized that there were passages in the Bible that implied that the Earth didn't move and the penalty for disagreeing with the Bible could be severe. He was careful to give his publication only to a small circle of fellow scientists who could be trusted.

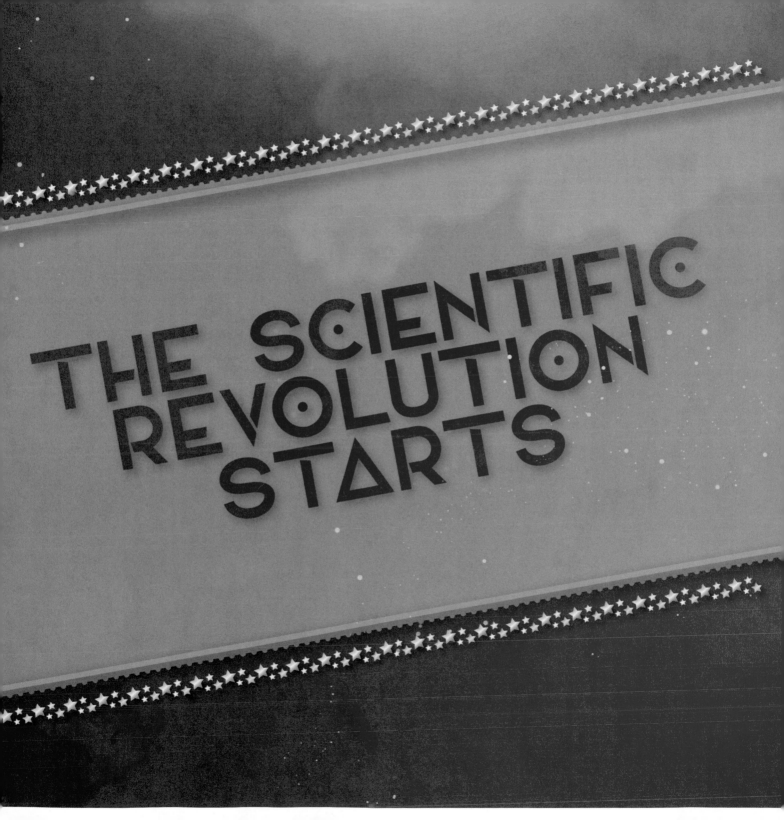

NICOLAI CO
PERNICI TORINENSIS
DE REVOLVTIONIBVS ORBI-
um coelestium, Libri VI.

.Habes in hoc opere iam recens nato, & ædito,
studiose lector, Motus stellarum, tam fixarum,
quàm erraticarum, cum ex ueteribus, tum etiam
ex recentibus obseruationibus restitutos: & no-
uis insuper ac admirabilibus hypothesibus or-
natos. Habes etiam Tabulas expeditissimas, ex
quibus eosdem ad quoduis tempus quàm facilli
me calculare poteris. Igitur eme, lege, fruere.

Ἀγεωμέτρητος ὐδὶς ἐσίτω.

Norimbergæ apud Ioh. Petreium,
Anno M. D. XLIII.

DE REVOLUTIONIBUS ORBIUM
COELESTIUM TITLE PAGE, ORIGINAL
1543 NUREMBERG EDITION

Copernicus had gathered enough material to emphasize his claims by 1532 in a manuscript called *De revolutionibus orbium coelestium*, which essentially means the revolutions of the heavenly spheres. He was still careful in sharing it with others, but word began to leak out about his theories. Seven years passed and his masterwork still wasn't officially published.

Then, something happened that changed things. A German astronomer and mathematician called Georg Joachim Rheticus came to work with Copernicus as his apprentice. Rheticus thought that Copernicus's manuscript was far too important to keep under wraps so he convinced him to let him take it to Germany to be published.

GEORG JOACHIM RHETICUS

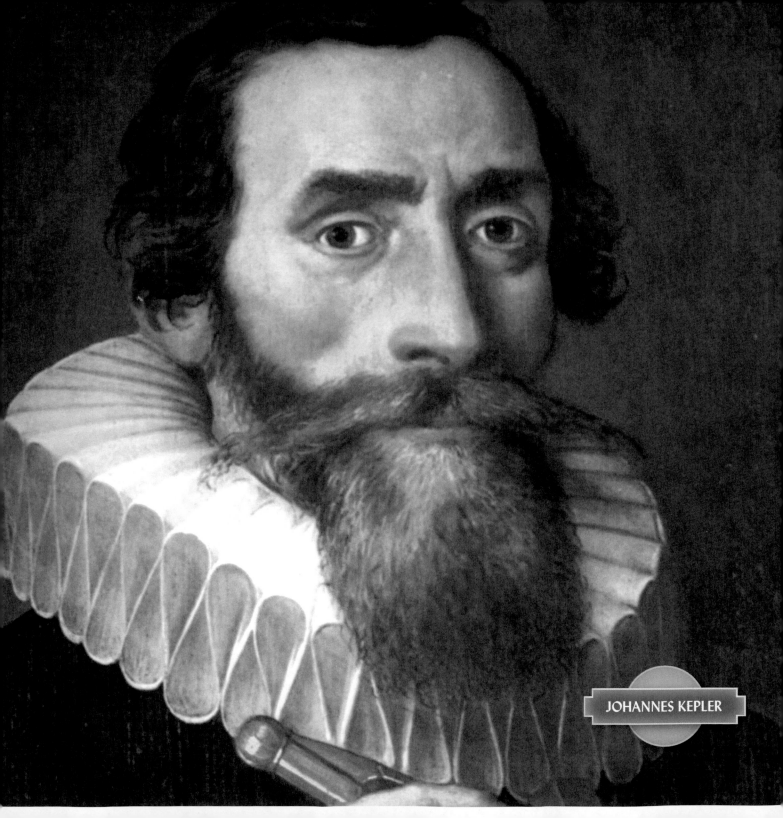

JOHANNES KEPLER

Legend has it that Copernicus received a copy of the book on his deathbed in 1543. It became the new reference work for the following generations of astronomers like Galileo Galilei and Johannes Kepler. His ideas sparked the beginning of the scientific revolution. As Copernicus's theories continued to spread, the Catholic Church claimed that the book was heresy and it was banned in 1616. Although the Church was very powerful in those days, they didn't manage to wipe out his theories.

Today it is a known fact that the planets including the Earth travel around the Sun. In 2010, Copernicus's grave was reburied and his current tombstone depicts a bright golden sun with planets traveling around it. Despite all this, there are some people who refuse to believe that the Sun doesn't travel around the Earth!

GRAVE OF NICOLAUS COPERNICUS
IN FROMBORK CATHEDRAL

NICOLAUS COPERNICUS,
POLISH ASTRONOMER

SUMMARY

For thousands of years, people believed that the Earth was at the center as the planets made their orbits. In fact, people thought that the Earth was at the center of the known universe. This belief had become so ingrained that it was almost thought of as a religious principle. However, little by little the science of the ancient Greeks was found to be incorrect.

Copernicus made careful astronomical observations and put forth a theory that the Earth wasn't positioned at the center at all. Instead, he correctly claimed that the Sun was at the central point and that the planets, including the Earth, revolved around the Sun. The term "solar system" wasn't used on a regular basis until 1704.

Awesome! Now that you've learned about the life and theories of Nicolaus Copernicus you may want to read more about the solar system in the Baby Professor book, *What is The Solar System? Astronomy Book for Kids | Children's Astronomy Books.*

Visit

www.SpeedyBookStore.com

To view and download free content
on your favorite subject and browse
our catalog of new and exciting
books for readers of all ages.

Made in the USA
Monee, IL
29 November 2022